EUNOIA

CHRISTIAN BÖK

COACH HOUSE BOOKS

Published with generous assistance from the Canada Council
for the Arts and the Ontario Arts Council. Coach House Books
also appreciates the support of the Government of Canada
through the Book Publishing Industry Development Program.

    Canada Council   Conseil des Arts   ONTARIO ARTS COUNCIL   Canadä
                     for the Arts   du Canada   CONSEIL DES ARTS DE L'ONTARIO

LIBRARY AND ARCHIVES CANADA
CATALOGUING IN PUBLICATION DATA

Bök, Christian, 1966–
    Eunoia / Christian Bök – New ed.

Poems.
ISBN 978-1-55245-225-7

    I. Title.

PS8553.04727E86 2009   c811'.54   C2009-904269-x

Source of my being, and my life's support!
Eunoia *call'd in this celestial Court.*

William Hayley
The Triumphs of Temper (1781)

*for the new
ennui in you*

EUNOIA

OISEAU

EUNOIA

CHAPTER A

for Hans Arp

Awkward grammar appals a craftsman. A Dada bard as daft as Tzara damns stagnant art and scrawls an alpha (a slapdash arc and a backward zag) that mars all stanzas and jams all ballads (what a scandal). A madcap vandal crafts a small black ankh – a hand-stamp that can stamp a wax pad and at last plant a mark that sparks an *ars magna* (an abstract art that charts a phrasal anagram). A pagan skald chants a dark saga (a Mahabharata), as a papal cabal blackballs all annals and tracts, all dramas and psalms: Kant and Kafka, Marx and Marat. A law as harsh as a *fatwa* bans all paragraphs that lack an A as a standard hallmark.

Hassan Abd al-Hassad, an Agha Khan, basks at an ashram – a Taj Mahal that has grand parks and grass lawns, all as vast as parklands at Alhambra and Valhalla. Hassan can, at a handclap, call a vassal at hand and ask that all staff plan a bacchanal – a gala ball that has what pagan charm small galas lack. Hassan claps, and (*tah-dah*) an Arab lass at a swank spa can draw a man's bath and wash a man's back, as Arab lads fawn and hang, athwart an altar, amaranth garlands as fragrant as attar – a balm that calms all angst. A dwarf can flap a palm branch that fans a fat maharajah. A naphtha lamp can cast a calm warmth.

Hassan asks that a vassal grant a man what manna a man wants: Alaskan crabs, alfalfa salad and kasha, Malahat clams, lasagna pasta and salsa. Hassan wants Kalamata shawarma, cassabananas and taramasalata. Hassan gnaws at a calf flank and chaws at a lamb shank, as a charman chars a black bass and salts a bland carp. Hassan scarfs back gravlax and sprats, crawdad and prawns, balks at Parma ham, and has, as a snack, *canard à l'ananas sans safran.* Hassan asks that a vassal grant a man jam tarts and bananas, jam flans and casabas, halva, pappadam and challah, babka, fasnacht and baklava.

Hassan can watch cancan gals cha-cha-cha, as brass bands blat jazz razzmatazz (what a class act). Rapt fans at a bandstand can watch jazzbands that scat a waltz and a samba. Fans clap as a fat-cat jazzman and a bad-ass bassman blab gangsta rap – a gangland fad that attacks what Brahms and Franck call art: a Balkan czardas, a Tartar tandava (sarabands that can charm a saltant chap at a *danza*). Bach can craft a Catalan sardana that attracts *l'Afghan chantant à l'amant dansant*. A sax drawls tantaras (all A-flats and an A-sharp): *fa-la-la-la-la*. A maraca rasps cantatas. A lass as sad as a swan twangs a glass harp.

Hassan can ask that a barman at a bar tap a cask and draw a man a draft (half a dram, a glass): marc, grappa and armagnac, malt, arrack and schnapps. Gangs that act as crass as Harvard grads at a frat (Gamma Kappa Lambda) clack tankards and gawk at a gal, as a gal dabs at black mascara. Rash lads that harass vamps and bawds catcall a brash tramp: 'caramba – what a tart'. A bacchant lad asks a madam (as drachmas pass hands): 'what carnal acts can a man transact?' A gal can grab a man's balls and wank a man's shaft; a man can grasp a gal's bra and spank a gal's ass. A clasp snaps apart, and a scant shawl falls.

Hassan wants a catnap and grabs, as a calmant, hash, grass and smack, khat, ganja and tabac – an amalgam that can spark a pharmacal flashback. Hassan falls slack, arms asprawl, and has a nap that spawns dark phantasmata. Satan stands back, aback a damask arras, and draws a fractal mandala – a charm that can trap what a Cathar savant calls an 'astral avatar' (part man, part bat – all fang and claw) – a phantasm that can snarl and gnash at a carcass. A fantast chants 'abracadabra' as a mantra, wags a wand, and (*zap*) a sandglass cracks. A hag as mad as Cassandra warns a shah that bad karma attracts phantasmal cataclasms.

Hassan balks at all sacral tasks – a mass at Sabbath, a fast at Ramadan: 'what Kabbalah and Brahmana can match blackjack and baccarat?' Hassan brags that a crackajack champ at cards lacks what knack Hassan has at craps. A cardsharp, smart at canasta, has a scam: mark a pack, palm a jack. (A cardmatch can act as a starchart that maps *fata arcana*.) A shah hazards all cash, stands pat and calls. A fatal pall wracks a casbah, as a charlatan fans a grandslam hand ('damn, darn, drat' rants a braggart). A rascal salaams and thanks Allah that a bank can award a man a stash that dwarfs what alms a raj can amass.

Hassan drafts a Magna Carta and asks that a taxman pass a Tax Act – a cash grab that can tax all farmland and grant a dastard at cards what hard cash Hassan lacks. Hassan asks that an apt draftsman map what ranchland a ranchhand can farm: all grasslands and pampas, all marshlands and swamps, flatlands and savannahs (standard badlands that spawn chaparral and crabgrass). Hassan asks that all farmhands at farms plant flax and award Hassan, as a tax, half what straw a landsman can stash at a barn. A ranchman at a ranch warns *campagnards* that a shah has spat at hard-and-fast laws that ban cadastral graft.

Hassan can tax a Saharan caravan that carts packs and sacks past bazaars at Aswan and Rabat, Basra and Dakar. Stalls at all marts hawk Baccarat glass. Stands at all malls hawk Macassar brass. A haggard almsman can drag a handcart and hawk glass jars (racks and racks): agar-agar – dammar lac and balsam sap (half a franc, a flask). A drab washman, half-clad at a washstand, can wash afghans and caftans, sandals and tabards, as a ragman darns rags and hawks rag-tag garb: slacks, pajamas and pants, scarfs, cravats and spats. A chapman at a standard hatstand can hawk panama hats, canvas caps and tartan tams.

Hassan can tax all banal trash that vagrants at a plaza pawn and swap: ant farms and lava lamps, rat traps and lawn darts – chaff and draff that jampacks all trashcans. A trashman and a scrapman can pawn scrap parts: fans, amps and a dashlamp, rads, cams and a camshaft, gas tanks and clamps, car jacks and straps, hand-cranks that can crank a crankshaft. A lampman at a lampstand can hawk Argand lamps (all brands): arc lamps and gas lamps, flashlamps that flash at half a watt. A sawman can hawk all handsaws and hacksaws, all bandsaws and backsaws, sharp saws that saw apart a flat-sawn plank.

Hassan at Arab talks can canvass all satraps and ask that Arab banks back what grand plans Hassan has (dams and canals at Panama, arks and wharfs at Havana – tasks that, as a drawback, warrant what Hassan calls 'a harsh tax plan'). Hassan lacks tact, and (alas) a rajah's blatant sarcasm sparks a flagrant backlash as rampant as a vandal's wrath. Hassan grandstands at a grandstand, as all thralls lash back, wag placards and rant a clamant rant. Arrant gangs clash and start brawls that trash rattan cabanas (what a fracas). A maharajah asks that a hangman hang all bastards and laggards that a lawman can catch.

Hassan can watch, aghast, as databanks at NASDAQ graph hard data and chart a NASDAQ crash – a sharp fall that alarms staff at a Manhattan bank. Hassan acts fast, ransacks cashbags at a mad dash, and grabs what bank drafts a bank branch at Casablanca can cash: marks, rands and bahts. Hassan asks that an adman draft a want ad that can hawk what canvas art Hassan has (a Cranach, a Cassatt and a Chagall). Hassan can fast-talk a chap at a watchstand and pawn a small watch that has, as a watchglass, a star *padparadschah* (half a grand, a carat). A shah can pack a bag, flag a cab and scram, catch-as-catch-can.

Hassan has a dacha at Kazakhstan, and at a small shack Hassan can hatch a dark plan. Hassan wants back what past landmass a shah has had (vacant tracts that span as far as Khanabad and Ashkhabad, Kandahar and Samarkand – landmarks that Kazakh anarchs smash apart and sack). Hassan can scan an atlas that maps Madagascar and all lands afar: Java, Malta and Japan, Chad, Ghana and Qatar, Canada and Lapland, Rwanda and Malabar. Hassan can scan an almanac that charts facts and stats at Dallas, Savannah and Atlanta (Kansas, Arkansas and Alabama). Hassan asks that banks at Warsaw and Gdansk fax Hassan a fax.

Hassan can start a war. Hassan marshalls an armada that can attack Javan wharfs at Jakarta. Hassan asks that all sampans trawl canals and chart thalassal hazards (sandbanks that can strand a small bark, cataracts that can thwart a balsa raft); catamarans as fast as narwhals dash past a sandbar and ram all naval craft that lack ballast at landfall. Masts snap. Spars warp. A gangplank cracks as backwash slams a carrack and swamps a canvas tarp (*splash, splash*). A raftsman and a hatchman bark 'avast' and clamp a hatch, as all hands man a capstan and tack landward, hard abaft. A damp flag flaps at half-mast.

Hassan can watch as all hands land a small warcraft and camp at a lava sandflat – a basalt strand that has tar sands as black as magma ash. Wasps and gnats swarm as all hands stack sandbags and start a spartan camp. A campman, smart at campcraft, can spark a match and warm an ashpan that thaws what hardtack a clan wants: bran mash and lard, spam hash and salt, ballpark franks and flapjack stacks (all starch and fat). A packman at camp packs a backpack, a knapsack and a packsack. A watchman stands watch, as all ranks at dawn act as pawns that can marshall adamant brawn and march a harsh warpath.

Hassan can watch as a marksman tracks a stag, a hart and a fawn, and at last bags a ram (a bwana as smart as Tarzan can trap all mammals: alpacas and llamas, caracals and pandas, aardvarks that can catch larval ants). Hawks and larks dart past tamaracks, as jackdaws and mallards flap past catalpas and land athwart a larch (sparhawks and caracaras scrawk at blackcaps and avadavats). A bantam jacamar can stand athwart a jacaranda branch and catch all scarabs that gnaw at sassafras bark. A jackal stalks an addax. A Manx cat nabs a pack rat. A black asp crawls past a sawgrass marsh that has algal tarns.

Macaws caw as a phalanx tramps past a tall alp (a stark crag that dwarfs all scarps and chasms), and at a dark pass all ranks halt, stand fast and attack a vast barracks that has ramparts and catwalks. A Spartan axman as stalwart as Ajax grabs an ax and hacks at a swart clansman: *whack, whack.* A Rwandan man-at-arms grasps an atlatl and casts a fatal shaft that can stab a grand marshall. A Slav warman as gallant as Galahad (and D'Artagnan) clasps a scabbard and draws a katana that can smash a man's brassards and slash a man's flancards. A sharp hand adz can bash a man's arms and gash a man's gams: *swack, swack.*

Alarms clang as a radarman tracks an attack craft that can jam radar and dart past flak at half a Mach: *ack-ack-ack, rat-tat-tat.* Vaward attacks blast apart hangars and tarmacs: *blam, blam.* Plasma blasts scald asphalt; napalm blasts parch macadam (glass shards act as haphazard abradants that sandblast all landwrack). Tanks clank and clack, as halftracks attack flatcars and tramcars: *bang, bang.* Cars and vans crash. A Mazda hatchback and a Saab smack a tram: *wham, wham.* A mad labman at a lab crafts an anthrax gas that can waft past all walls at a stalag and harm war camps that lack standard gas masks.

Hassan gags and has an asthma attack – a catarrh as fatal as lhasa and hanta. Cramps as sharp as darts and barbs jab and jag at gastral tracts. Carpal pangs gnarl a man's hands and cramp a man's palms. Hassan asks that a shaman abstract a talc cataplasm that can thwart a blatant rash (raw scars that can scar a man's scalp and gall a man's glans: *scratch, scratch*). A warm saltbath can blanch all plantar warts and stanch all palatal scabs. A transplant can patch a basal gland. A bald shah barfs and farts as a labman bawls: 'plasma, stat' (alas, alack: a shah has a grand mal spasm and, *ahh*, gasps a schwa, as a last gasp).

CHAPTER E

for René Crevel

Enfettered, these sentences repress free speech. The text deletes selected letters. We see the revered exegete reject metred verse: the sestet, the tercet – even *les scènes élevées en grec*. He rebels. He sets new precedents. He lets cleverness exceed decent levels. He eschews the esteemed genres, the expected themes – even *les belles lettres en vers*. He prefers the perverse French esthetes: Verne, Péret, Genet, Perec – hence, he pens fervent screeds, then enters the street, where he sells these letterpress newsletters, three cents per sheet. He engenders perfect newness wherever we need fresh terms.

Relentless, the rebel peddles these theses, even when vexed peers deem the new precepts 'mere dreck'. The plebes resent newer verse; nevertheless, the rebel perseveres, never deterred, never dejected, heedless, even when hecklers heckle the vehement speeches. We feel perplexed whenever we see these excerpted sentences. We sneer when we detect the clever scheme – the emergent repetend: the letter E. We jeer; we jest. We express resentment. We detest these depthless pretenses – these present-tense verbs, expressed pell-mell. We prefer genteel speech, where sense redeems senselessness.

Westerners revere the Greek legends. Versemen retell the represented events, the resplendent scenes, where, hellbent, the Greek freemen seek revenge whenever Helen, the new-wed empress, weeps. Restless, she deserts her fleece bed where, detested, her wedded regent sleeps. When she remembers Greece, her seceded demesne, she feels wretched, left here, bereft, her needs never met. She needs rest; nevertheless, her demented fevers render her sleepless (her sleeplessness enfeebles her). She needs help; nevertheless, her stressed nerves render her cheerless (her cheerlessness enfetters her).

Whenever Helen feels these stresses, she trembles. She frets. Her helplessness vexes her. She feels depressed (even when her cleverest beekeepers fetch her the freshest sweets). She feels neglected (even when her shrewdest gemseekers fetch her the greenest jewels). She regrets her wretchedness, her dejectedness; nevertheless, she keeps her deepest regrets secret. She never lets herself express her *echt Weltschmerz.* She never vents spleen. She feels tense whenever she keeps her vehemence repressed; hence, she seeks lewd revelment (*les fêtes de ses rêves*), where revellers lend her cheer.

Whenever Helen dresses herself *en fête,* her sewn vestments reflect her resplendence. Whenever she needs new ensembles, her sempstresses sew her ten velveteen dresses, then hem her red checkered sleeves. Her jewellers bevel gems, then bejewel her sceptre (*l'emblème des régences célestes*). Her eldest helpers preen her tresses; then her effete servers serve her dessert. The empress prefers sweetened preserves; hence, her serfs get her the best gels ever jelled: *les pêches gelées* – blended sherbet, served fresh. The scented dessert smells even sweeter when served ere the sweetness melts.

Whenever Helen needs effervescent refreshments, she tells her expert brewer: 'brew me the best beer ever brewed'. Whenever she lets her fermenters ferment the perfect beer, revellers wreck the kegs, then feed themselves the lees. Retchers retch; belchers belch. Jesters express extreme glee. Wenches then sell these lewd perverts sex. The lechers leer whenever svelte negresses tempt the perverted gentlemen. The empress revels. She sheds her velvet dress; then she lets repellent men pet her tender flesh. Her lewdness renders even these lechers speechless. She resembles the lewdest jezebel.

Whenever Helen seeks these perverse excesses, her regretted deeds depress her; hence, Helen beseeches Ceres (the blessèd Demeter): 'let sweet Lethe bless me, lest these recent events be remembered' – then the empress feeds herself fermented hempseed, her preferred nepenthe. Whenever she chews these hell-bred seeds, the hempweed skews her senses. The hemp, when chewed, lessens her tenseness (hence, she feels serene); nevertheless, the weed, when needed, renders her dependent. She enters the deepest sleep – the nether sphere, where sleepers delve the secret depths.

Whenever Helen sleeps, her essence enters the ether – the deep well, where she feels herself descend deeper, deeper. Her descent seems endless; nevertheless, she lets herself be swept wherever the gentle breeze sweeps her. She regresses. She sees levels never seen except when men enter the seven hells (*les enfers éternels des gens désespérés*): the fell dens where beetles creep, the deep fens where leeches dwell – there, the sewers reek. The stench repels; nevertheless, the sleek green eels feed themselves the excrement (the expelled feces, the excreted dregs); then the serpents breed themselves.

Whenever Helen enters Hell's deepest recesses, she sees Hell's meekest dwellers. She meets the repenters, never redeemed. She greets her decedent elders. The elder seers, when greeted, tell her: 'repent, repent – never let the tempters here tempteth thee' – then these helpless wretches tell her three spells best kept secret, lest the tempted empress reverse these hexes, then set free demented spectres, held here, bespelled. The three spells, when reversed, sever these hexed fetters; hence, the berserk efreets, when freed, screech 'hell's bells', then flee these endless deserts, where the embers swelter.

Whenever Helen sleeps, her fevered rest meekens her; hence, she re-emerges enfeebled – her strength, expended; her reserves, depleted. The extended fevers, when severe, entrench her enfeeblement. She clenches her teeth, then exerts herself; nevertheless, she feels strengthless (her meek self rendered even meeker). Her strengthlessness dejects her. She sneezes; she wheezes – then she spews phlegm; nevertheless, she rejects her self-centred meekness. She begs her defenders: 'defend me'; she begs her redeemers: 'redeem me' – then she decrees: 'never desert me – lend me renewed verve'.

Hermes, the messenger, tells her the news: 'Thebes sends the fleet'. The Hellene freemen seek redress. The steersmen steer the xebecs between steep, sheer clefts, where reefs prevent sheltered berth; there, the tempests whelm the decks, then wreck the keels – the helms, left crewless whenever the elements beset these crewmen. The December sleet drenches the tethered nets, then threshes the fettered pegs; hence, the deckmen wedge the kevels, then check the kedges; nevertheless, these vessels teeter. The lee sheets, when drenched, get reft, then rent. The wheelmen, when wet, wrest the wheel.

Mermen help these helmsmen berth the wrecked vessels; then the Greek crews erect well-defended shelters wherever the fleet gets berthed. Men erect mess tents, then feed sheds. The settlers dredge the kelp beds, then extend the levees. The wreckers heft sledges; then the hewers hew the evergreens when the evergreens get felled. The trestlemen erect trestles; the smeltermen erect smelters. Men smelt the steel; then the deftest welders weld the tempered sheet steel wherever men screw the screws. The best sled ever hewn gets erected. The shell, when welded, resembles the fleetest steed.

Greek schemers respect shrewdness; hence, the shrewd rebels enter the sled's secret recess, the sled's nested crèche, where these few men keep themselves secreted. Then the sled gets sent wherever the nemeses dwell; there, the Greek pretenders pretend: 'the well-hewn steed represents the perfect present'. The wedded regent sees these presenters present the steed; hence, he decrees: 'the plebes express excellent reverence'. He never detects the pretense; hence, he errs when he lets the presented steed enter the crenelled keep. The rebels never get detected when the keep gets entered.

Greek schemers seek egress *en ténèbres,* then enter the melee – the welter where berserk tempers seethe whenever men's mettle, then men's fettle, gets tested; there, the Greek berserkers sever men's thews, then shred men's flesh. When the rebels beset defended trenches, the defenders retrench themselves, then strengthen the embedded defences. The strengthened deterrence deters the rebels; nevertheless, these men esteem relentlessness; hence, the rebels expend themselves, then reject détente. We see them repel retrenched defencemen, then render the bested men defenceless.

Épées, when hefted, skewer the fencers; then wrestlers wrestle these skewered men (men's knees get threshed; men's necks get wrenched). Deft fletchers whet steel-edged reeds, then fletch these whetted skewers. When the helmeted men get pelted, the slender needles (*les fléchettes*) dent the crested helmets. The steel vests deflect even these keen edges; nevertheless, the steel sheen gets etched, then dented. The deserters defect. The men flee these entrenchments, where lepers get trench fever; there, legless men bleed. The welts fester. The severed members, strewn helter-skelter, redden the cerements.

Bells knell when the keep gets levelled; then Greek rebels cheer when Helen enters her Greek temple (the steepled glebe where jewelled steeples shelter her ephebes); there, the reverends bless the freed empress. The Greek sects revere her gentleness, her tenderness; hence, these prefects help her seek self-betterment. The zen seers tell her: 'greed begets greed – never be self-centred: be selfless'. She defers. Her deference seems reverent. The empress kneels, then keens her vespers. The pewter censer spews the sweetest peppered scent. She feels refreshed; she feels perfected.

Helen remembers Crete – the Eden where senescent shepherds (*les bergers des bêtes*) herd bellwether sheep; there, Helen sees the pebbled steppes (the eskers where chert scree bestrews the ledges). Helen treks wherever herdsmen trek. She sees the veldts where ewes, when fleeced, chew the sedges. She sees the glens, then the dells, where elk herds chew the vetch. She helps the herders erect fenced pens where hens peck feed; then she helps the shepherdesses sell the eggs. The sheepherders mend fences; the sheeptenders tend hedges. The sheepbreeders even breed steer, then geld them.

Helen sees the September breezes bend the elm trees (the perches where the egrets, then the grebes, perch themselves); there, the petrels, then the tercels, nest. Helen lets the geese peck seedlet kernels (except when ferrets pester the mews). The kestrels screech. The wrens peep: *tweet, tweet.* The terns keen: *cheep, cheep.* The peewee peetweets tweedle: *tweedledee, tweedledee.* The creeks wend between beech trees, then end where freshets feed the meres (there, the speckled perch teem; there, the freckled newts rest). The leverets, then the shrews, chew the nettles. The dew bedews the ferns.

When Vermeer sketches *les belles femmes de Delft,* he remembers Helen, then lends these sketches her extreme sereneness. When the sketchers (Erté, Ernst, Klee, Léger – even Bellmer) render *les événements des rêves,* these esthetes get felt pens, then sketch her presence. She seems sexless; nevertheless, men esteem her pert svelteness (her slender legs, her perfect feet); she represents perfectness; hence, we never see her defects (the speckles, the freckles). Men see her elven slenderness, then pledge themselves her serfs. She resembles Eve, the temptress – hence: *elle régne éternellement.*

CHAPTER I

for Dick Higgins

Writing is inhibiting. Sighing, I sit, scribbling in ink this pidgin script. I sing with nihilistic witticism, disciplining signs with trifling gimmicks – impish hijinks which highlight stick sigils. Isn't it glib? Isn't it chic? I fit childish insights within rigid limits, writing shtick which might instill priggish misgivings in critics blind with hindsight. I dismiss nitpicking criticism which flirts with philistinism. I bitch; I kibitz – griping whilst criticizing dimwits, sniping whilst indicting nitwits, dismissing simplistic thinking, in which philippic wit is still illicit.

Pilgrims, digging in shifts, dig till midnight in mining pits, chipping flint with picks, drilling schist with drills, striking it rich mining zinc. Irish firms, hiring micks whilst firing Brits, bring in smiths with mining skills: kilnwrights grilling brick in brickkilns, millwrights grinding grist in gristmills. Irish tinsmiths, fiddling with widgits, fix this rig, driving its drills which spin whirring drillbits. I pitch in, fixing things. I rig this winch with its wiring; I fit this drill with its piping. I dig this ditch, filling bins with dirt, piling it high, sifting it, till I find bright prisms twinkling with glitz.

Hiking in British districts, I picnic in virgin firths, grinning in mirth with misfit whims, smiling if I find birch twigs, smirking if I find mint sprigs. Midspring brings with it singing birds, six kinds (finch, siskin, ibis, tit, pipit, swift), whistling shrill chirps, trilling *chirr chirr* in high pitch. Kingbirds flit in gliding flight, skimming limpid springs, dipping wingtips in rills which brim with living things: krill, shrimp, brill – fish with gilt fins, which swim in flitting zigs. Might Virgil find bliss implicit in this primitivism? Might I mimic him in print if I find his writings inspiring?

Fishing till twilight, I sit, drifting in this birch skiff, jigging kingfish with jigs, bringing in fish which nip this bright string (its vivid glint bristling with stick pins). Whilst I slit this fish in its gills, knifing it, slicing it, killing it with skill, shipwrights might trim this jib, swinging it right, hitching it tight, riding brisk winds which pitch this skiff, tipping it, tilting it, till this ship in crisis flips. Rigging rips. Christ, this ship is sinking. Diving in, I swim, fighting this frigid swirl, kicking, kicking, swimming in it till I sight high cliffs, rising, indistinct in thick mists, lit with lightning.

Lightning blinks, striking things in its midst with blinding light. Whirlwinds whirl; driftwinds drift. Spindrift is spinning in thrilling whirligigs. Which blind spirit is whining in this whistling din? Is it this grim lich, which is writhing in its pit, lifting its lid with whitish limbs, rising, vivific, with ill will in its mind, victimizing kids timid with fright? If it is – which blind witch is midwifing its misbirth, binding this hissing djinni with witching spiritism? Is it this thin, sickish girl, twitching in fits, whilst writing things in spirit-writing? If it isn't – it is I; it is I ...

Lightning flicks its riding whip, blitzing this night with bright schisms. Sick with phthisis in this drizzling mist, I limp, sniffling, spitting bilic spit, itching livid skin (skin which is tingling with stinging pinpricks). I find this frigid drisk dispiriting; still, I fight its chilling windchill. I climb cliffs, flinching with skittish instincts. I might slip. I might twist this infirm wrist, crippling it, wincing whilst I bind it in its splint, cringing whilst I gird it in its sling; still, I risk climbing, sticking with it, striving till I find this rift, in which I might fit, hiding in it till winds diminish.

Minds grim with nihilism still find first light inspiring. Mild pink in tint, its shining twilight brings bright tidings which lift sinking spirits. With firm will, I finish climbing, hiking till I find this inviting inn, in which I might sit, dining. I thirst. I bid girls bring stiff drinks – gin fizz which I might sip whilst finishing this rich dish, nibbling its tidbits: ribs with wings in chili, figs with kiwis in icing. I swig citric drinks with vim, tippling kirsch, imbibing it till, giggling, I flirt with girlish virgins in miniskirts: *wink, wink.* I miss living in sin, pinching thighs, kissing lips pink with lipstick.

Slick pimps, bribing civic kingpins, distill gin in stills, spiking drinks with illicit pills which might bring bliss. Whiz kids in silk-knit shirts script films in which slim girls might strip, jiggling tits, wiggling hips, inciting wild shindigs. Twin siblings in bikinis might kiss rich bigwigs, giving this prim prig his wish, whipping him, tickling him, licking his limp dick till, rigid, his prick spills its jism. Shit! This ticklish victim is trifling with kink. Sick minds, thriving in kinship with pigs, might find insipid thrills in this filth. This flick irks critics. It is swinish; it is piggish. It stinks.

Thinking within strict limits is stifling. Whilst Viking knights fight griffins, I skirmish with this riddling sphinx (this sigil – I). I print lists, filing things (kin with kin, ilk with ilk), inscribing this distinct sign, listing things in which its imprint is intrinsic. I find its missing links, divining its implicit tricks. I find it whilst skindiving in Fiji; I find it whilst picnicking in Linz. I find it in Inniskillin; I find it in Mississippi. I find it whilst skiing in Minsk. (Is this intimism civilizing if Klimt limns it, if Liszt lilts it?) I sigh; I lisp. I finish writing this writ, signing it, kind sir: NIHIL DICIT, FINI.

CHAPTER O

for Yoko Ono

Loops on bold fonts now form lots of words for books. Books form cocoons of comfort – tombs to hold bookworms. Profs from Oxford show frosh who do postdocs how to gloss works of Wordsworth. Dons who work for proctors or provosts do not fob off school to work on crosswords, nor do dons go off to dorm rooms to loll on cots. Dons go crosstown to look for bookshops known to stock lots of top-notch goods: cookbooks, workbooks – room on room of how-to books for jocks (how to jog, how to box), books on pro sports: golf or polo. Old colophons on schoolbooks from schoolrooms sport two sorts of logo: oblong whorls, rococo scrolls – both on worn morocco.

Monks who vow to do God's work go forth from donjons of monkhood to show flocks lost to God how God's word brooks no crooks who plot to do wrong. Folks who go to Sodom kowtow to Moloch, so God drops H-bombs of horror onto poor townsfolk, most of whom mock Mormon proofs of godhood. Folks who do not follow God's norms word for word woo God's scorn, for God frowns on fools who do not conform to orthodox protocol. Whoso honors no cross of dolors nor crown of thorns doth go on, forsooth, to sow worlds of sorrow. Lo! No Song of Solomon comforts Job or Lot, both of whom know for whom gongs of doom doth toll. Oh, *mondo doloroso.*

Porno shows folks lots of sordor – zoom-shots of Björn Borg's bottom or Snoop Dogg's crotch. Johns who don condoms for blowjobs go downtown to Soho to look for pornshops known to stock lots of lowbrow schlock – off-color porn for old boors who long to drool onto color photos of cocks, boobs, dorks or dongs. Homos shoot photos of footlong schlongs. Blond trollops who don go-go boots flop pompoms nonstop to do promos for floorshows. Wow! Hot blonds who doff cotton frocks show off soft bosoms. Hot to trot, two blonds who smooch now romp on cold wood floors for crowds of morons, most of whom hoot or howl: *whoop, whoop.*

Blond showfolk who do soft porn go to boomtowns to look for work on photo shoots. Molls who hobnob from mob boss to mob boss croon solos from old torchsongs. Molls who do so do so *molto sordo* – too slow for most crowds to follow, so most crowds scoff: *boo, boo.* Folks who do not know how to plot common chords for rock songs or folk songs soon look for good songbooks on how to do so. Folks too cool to go to sock hops go to Woodstock rock shows to do pot, not to foxtrot to Motown rondos of pop, bop or doo-wop. Congo bongos throb to voodoo hoodoo; tom-toms for powwows go *boom, boom.* Gongs go *bong.* Kotos go *bonk.* Horns honk: *toot, toot.*

Folks from Kokomo do lots of shrooms (not snow, not blow – no form of hops). Folks who long to prolong moods of torpor do Zoloft or nod off on two drops of chloroform. Goofs who goof off go off to poolrooms to jolt down lots of good strong bock from Coors or Stroh. Most tosspots who toss down jolts of Grolsch do so to drown sorrows. Poor sots, blotto on two shots of scotch, go loco for old port or hot grog. Lots of hobos who do odd jobs for food go off to work to work on jobs no boss stoops to do – jog brooms of soot, mop floors of loos. Old coots, known to go to grogshops for snorts of wormwood hooch, go on to mooch dogfood from dogs.

Snobs who go to Bonn for bonbons know how to shop for good food: go to Moncton for cod, go to Concord for lox. Cooks who know how to cook *coq d'or* cook *cochon d'Ormont* or *cochon d'Orloff,* not pork chops or pork hocks. Cooks who do not know how to cook posh food do not opt to shop for lots of tools: no woks, spoons or forks, no pots, crocks or bowls. Cooks from Foochow or Soochow chow down on two sorts of broth: oolong or wonton. Folks from Stockholm scoff down bowls of borscht. Folks too poor to chow down on *bon porc* or *coq gros* wolf down corncobs or corndogs. Moms cook hotdogs for tots who chomp on orts of popcorn.

Scows from London go to Moscow, not to Boston, to drop off bolts of mothproof cloth: wool for long johns, wool for work socks. Moors from Morocco, not from Kowloon, go to Oporto to drop off two sorts of orlon floss (both sold to commonfolk, most of whom know how to do clothwork on looms): spools of cord (for hooks to hook), spools of woof (for combs to comb). Folks who work on looms knot knots to form cloth goods for showrooms to show: cotton shorts or cotton smocks – lots of togs for fops who go from shop to shop to look for thong gowns, now worn to proms. Folks who don ponchos for comfort don boots or clogs to go for strolls on downtown docks.

Brown logbooks show how scows from Norfolk go from port to port to stow on docks tons of hotchpotch goods: tools from workrooms, props from workshops (cogs for motors, rods for rotors) – box on box of foolproof clocks, row on row of clockwork robots. Scows from Toronto tow lots of logs thrown onto pontoons: tons of softwood, tons of cordwood – block on block of wood good for woodwork: boxwood, bowwood, dogwood, logwood (most sorts of wood sold to workfolks who work for old woodshops). Holds hold loot from Hong Kong or gold from Fort Knox. Old stockrooms stock lots of shopworn dross: doorknobs for doors, lockworks for locks.

Dhows from Colombo confront monsoons – strong storms known to slosh spoom onto prows of sloops. Folks who row old scows to cross floods of froth do not row scows worn down from wood rot (for most dolts who do so go forth, shorn of control, to rock, to roll, on storm-blown bobs of cork – now blown to or fro, now blown on or off, most known plots to known ports): *whoosh, whoosh*. Moms who sob for lost sons blow conch horns to honor poor fools who, thrown from port bows, go down, down, down (*oh no*) to drown – lost for good, now food for worms. Pods of octopods swoop down onto schools of cod to look for food: *swoosh, swoosh*.

Cold stormfronts from snowstorms blow snow onto fjords north of Oslo. Most storms howl for months: frost snows onto woods; froth blows onto rocks. From now on, snowplows plow snow. Cool brooks flow from grottos, down oxbows, to form pools or ponds. Long fronds of moonwort, known to grow from offshoot growths of rootstock, grow on moss bogs of sod. Soft blossoms of snowdrop now bloom on moors. Soon fog, not smog, rolls off old lochs onto boondocks of phlox. Lots of frogs hop from rock to rock: 'frog, pond, plop'. Cows *moo-moo* to foghorns. Dogs *bow-wow* to moonglow. Most loons coo soft coos: *coo, coo.* Hoot owls hoot: *hoo, hoo.*

Brown storks flock to brooks to look for schools of smolt or schools of snook. Wolf dogs (*los lobos*) prowl woods or moors to look for spoor of woodfowl or moorfowl. Most sorts of fox go off to snoop for coops known to hold woodcocks or moorcocks. Zoos known to stock zoomorphs (crocs or komodos, coons or bonobos) show off odd fowl: condors, hoopoos, flocks of owls or loons (not flocks of rocs or dodos). Most sloths, too slow to scoot from log to log, loll on mossgrown knolls of cottonwood to chomp on bollworms. Most worms molt from soft pods of cocoons to form broods of moths (two sorts: wood moth or moon moth): *shoo,* moth, *shoo.*

Scots from hogtowns or cowtowns work from cock-crow to moondown – to chop down woodlots, to plow down cornrows. Folks who work from morn to noon throw down slop to hogs or corn to sows. Most workfolk who sow crops of broomcorn grow corn crops sown from lots of cowflop compost (blobs of poo or globs of goo). From two o'clock on, workfolk groom colts born of broncos. Most cowfolk who hold onto cowprods to prod two sorts of ox (shorthorn or pronghorn) flog no shod ox sold to tow oxplows. Most honchos who own lots of longhorns on hoof shoot cows known to host cowpox. Dogs growl. Hogs snort. Most rooks or crows roost on rooftops.

Crooks who con folks go door to door to show folks lots of books on how to boost longshot growth of hot-shot stocks or low-cost bonds. Crooks who do so fob off fool's gold onto fools. Crowds of droogs, who don workboots to stomp on downtrod hobos, go on to rob old folks, most of whom own posh co-op condos. Goons who shoot folks knock down doors, storm control rooms. Bronx cops do crowd control. Corps of shock-troops cordon off two blocks of shops to look for kooks who concoct knock-off bombs. Corps of storm-troops confront mobs of lowborn hoods, most of whom lob Molotov bombs to bomb pollbooths or tollbooths: *pow, pow – boom.*

Crowds of Ostrogoths who howl for blood go off on foot – to storm forts, to torch towns. Mongol troops, grown strong from bloodsport, loot strongholds of lords known to own tons of gold. Goths who lop off locks on doors of tombs spot no strongbox of loot – no gold, no boon – for Goths confront horrors too gross for words: gorgons from Mordor, kobolds from Chthon. Bold sons of Thor, god of storms, hold off, sword for sword, mobs of Morlocks – trolls who flood forth from bottommost worlds of rockbottom gloom. Orcs shoot bolts from crossbows. Lots of potshots, shot off from bows, mow down throngs of cohorts, most of whom swoon from loss of blood.

Goths who rob tombs confront old ghosts (most of whom prowl from ghost town to ghost town to spook poltroons). Lots of ghosts, who brood, forlorn, on moods of loss, howl for long-lost consorts – blond frows, sworn to honor fond vows of forsworn troth (now long forgot). Most consorts, too forlorn to long for comfort from sorrow, sob: *boohoo, boohoo* – so bozo clowns, who know not how to frown, don cox-combs, for pomp, for show, to spoof droll plots from books. Most fools who josh lords or mock snobs don hoods or cowls to do so (for wroth lords who scowl oft long to shoot folks who honor no form of snob-dom). Most fools go: 'oops, ow – oh, bollocks: *ho, ho*'.

Troop doctors who stop blood loss from torn colons or shot torsos go to Kosovo to work pro bono for poor commonfolk, most of whom confront horrors born of long pogroms. Good doctors who go to post-op to comfort folks look for sponsors to sponsor down-trod POWS from Lvov or Brno. Good doctors do months of work on blood flow to show how no form of pox (no protozoon, no sporozoon) clots blood from blood donors. Most Dogon, voodoo doctors, who splosh oxblood onto voodoo dolls, know how to concoct good mojo for octoroons from Togo. Folk doctors cook pots of bromo from roots of bloodwort or toothwort – common worts for common colds.

Profs who work for Komsomol go to Novgorod to work on robot bombs: H-bombs or N-bombs (two sorts of bloodshot horror for worlds of tomorrow). Most profs who know how to work control knobs on chronotrons shoot protons from cosmotrons to clock how long two photons glow. Orbs of phosphor throw off bolts of hot volts (googols of bosons from photoprotons of thoron). Lots of robots mold strong forms of boron for hot-rod motors (most sold to Ford, not to Volvo): *zoom, zoom – vroom.* Poof! Dots of color, blown off from blowtorch torchglow, scorch lots of moths (for moths oft bob from torch to torch). Most glowworms glow.

Profs who go to Knossos to look for books on Phobos or Kronos go on to jot down monophthongs (*kof* or *rho*) from two monoglot scrolls on Thoth, old god of Copts – both scrolls torn from hornbooks, now grown brown from mold. Profs who gloss works of Woolf, Gogol, Frost or Corot look for books from Knopf: *Oroonoko* or *Nostromo* – not *Hopscotch* (nor *Tlooth*). Profs who do schoolwork on Pollock look for photobooks on Orozco or Rothko (two tomfools who throw bold colors, blotch on blotch, onto tondos of dropcloth). Log onto Hotbot dotcom to look for books on who's who or wot's wot (for books of *bons mots* show folks lots of mottos to follow). How now brown cow.

CHAPTER U

for Zhu Yu

Kultur spurns Ubu – thus Ubu pulls stunts. Ubu shuns *Skulptur:* Uruk urns (plus busts), Zulu jugs (plus tusks). Ubu sculpts junk *für Kunst und Glück.* Ubu busks. Ubu drums drums, plus Ubu strums cruths (such hubbub, such ruckus): *thump, thump; thrum, thrum.* Ubu puns puns. Ubu blurts untruth: much bunkum (plus bull), much humbug (plus bunk) – but trustful schmucks trust such untruthful stuff; thus Ubu (cult guru) must bluff dumbstruck numbskulls (such chumps). Ubu mulcts surplus funds (trust funds plus slush funds). Ubu usurps much usufruct. Ubu sums up lump sums. Ubu trumps dumb luck.

Duluth dump trucks lurch, pull U-turns. Such trucks dump much undug turf: *clunk, clunk – thud.* Scum plus crud plugs up ducts; thus Ubu must flush such sulcus ruts. Sump pumps pump: *chuff, chuff.* Such pumps suck up mush plus muck – dung lumps (plus clumps), turd hunks (plus chunks): grugru grubs plus fungus slugs mulch up humus pulp. Ubu unplugs flux. Ubu scrubs up curbs; thus Ubu must brush up sulfur dust plus lugnut rust: *scuff, scuff.* Ubu burns unburnt mundungus. Ubu lugs stuff; Ubu tugs stuff. Ubu puts up fulcrums. Ubu puts up mud huts, but mugwumps shun such glum suburb slums: *tut, tut.*

Dutch smut churns up blushful succubus lusts; thus buff hunks plus hung studs must fuck lustful sluts: Ruth plus Lulu. Ubu struts. Ubu snuffs up drugs. Ubu hugs Ruth; thus Ruth purrs. Ubu untucks Ruth's muumuu; thus Ruth must untruss Ubu's tux. Ubu fluffs Lulu's tutu. Ubu cups Lulu's dugs; Ubu rubs Lulu's buns; thus Lulu must pull Ubu's pud. Ubu sucks Ruth's cunt; Ubu cuffs Ruth's butt. Ubu stuffs Ruth's bum (such fun). Ubu pumps Lulu's plush, sunburnt tush. Ubu humps Lulu's plump, upthrust rump. Ubu ruts. Ubu huffs; Ubu puffs. Ubu blurts: *push, push.* Ubu thrusts. Ubu bucks. Cum spurts. Ubu cums.

Ubu gulps up brunch: duck, hummus, nuts, fugu, bulgur, buns (crusts plus crumbs), blutwurst, brüh-wurst, spuds, curds, plums: *munch, munch.* Ubu sups. Ubu slurps rum punch. Ubu chugs full cups (plus mugs), full tubs (plus tuns): *glug, glug.* Ubu gluts up grub; thus Ubu's plump gut hurts. Ubu grunts: *ugh, ugh.* Ubu burps up mucus sputum. Ubu up-chucks lunch. Ubu slumps. Ubu sulks. Ubu shrugs. Ubu slurs drunk chums. Ubu snubs such drunks; thus curt churls cuss: 'shut up, Ubu, shut up'. Gruff punks club Ubu. Butch thugs drub Ubu. Ku-klux cults kung-fu punch Ubu. Rumdum bums bust up pubs.

Gulls churr: *ululu, ululu.* Ducks cluck. Bulls plus bucks run thru buckbrush; thus dun burrs clutch fur tufts. *Ursus* cubs plus *Lupus* pups hunt skunks. Curs skulk (such mutts lurk: *ruff, ruff*). Gnus munch kudzu. Lush shrubs bud; thus church nuns pluck uncut mums. Bugs hum: *buzz, buzz.* Dull susurrus gusts murmur hushful, humdrum murmurs: *hush, hush.* Dusk suns blush. Surf lulls us. Such scuds hurl up cumulus suds (*Sturm und Druck*) – furls unfurl: *rush, rush;* curls uncurl: *gush, gush.* Such tumult upturns unsunk hulls; thus gulfs crush us, *gulp,* dunk us – burst lungs succumb.

OISEAU

VOYELLES

by Arthur Rimbaud

A noir, E blanc, I rouge, U vert, O bleu: voyelles,
Je dirai quelque jour vos naissances latentes:
A, noir corset velu des mouches éclatantes
Qui bombinent autour des puanteurs cruelles,

Golfes d'ombre; E, candeurs des vapeurs et des tentes,
Lances des glaciers fiers, rois blancs, frissons d'ombelles;
I, pourpres, sang craché, rire des lèvres belles
Dans la colère ou les ivresses pénitentes;

U, cycles, vibrements divins des mers virides,
Paix des pâtis semés d'animaux, paix des rides
Que l'alchimie imprime aux grands fronts studieux;

O, suprême Clairon plein des strideurs étranges,
Silences traversés des [Mondes et des Anges]:
– O l'Oméga, rayon violet de [Ses] Yeux!

VOWELS

by Christian Bök

A black, E white, I red, U green, O blue: the vowels.
I will tell thee, one day, of thy newborn portents:
A, the black velvet cuirass of flies whose essence
commingles, abuzz, around the cruellest of smells,

Wells of shadow; E, the whitewash of mists and tents,
glaives of icebergs, albino kings, frostbit fennels;
I, the bruises, the blood spat from lips of damsels
who must laugh in scorn or shame, both intoxicants;

U, the waves, divine vibratos of verdant seas,
pleasant meadows rich with venery, grins of ease
which alchemy grants the visages of the wise;

O, the supreme Trumpeter of our strange sonnet –
quietudes crossed by another [World and Spirit]:
O, the Omega! – the violet raygun of [Her] Eyes …

PHONEMES

for Arthur Rimbaud

Phantoms, infernal,
without refuge or return – phonemes.

We will hark if such
resurgent souls ordain a dreamt verse:

A (offspring of perfect
murders, so unseen that stranglers

fulfill no crime, and thus
mourners must call the unjust schemes

overdoses); E (charmed
slumber that engulfs the sleepers,

cradled by dreamlike
Sirens who sing mankind forlorn themes);

I (corrupted archangel,
shriven when mercy redeems

all shadowy spectres
who plunder shipwrecked believers);

U (the Sphinx, beheld
by disciples, then by infidels:

a riddle that grieves
a king; a truth that crippled minstrels

must bewail in epics,
like staunch martyrs whom Furies spurn);

O (untempted Saint,
who lends this typewritten utterance

its fervency
– an endless cycle of perseverance).

O, how the Bards
abolish symbols, when the letters burn …

VEILS

for Arthur Rimbaud

Anywhere near blank rage
you veer, oblivial.

Jade array, calico azure
evanescent talents.

Unaware, corrosives flow
to my shackled hand.

Key bombing an auto tour
to paint her colour.

Gulfs of amber contours
evaporate the tint.

Linseed glass or oblong
freezing dumbbells.

Upper pressing cashiers
do deliver verbals.

Dance the clear, elusive
rinse of paintings.

Icicle fibre meant divine
daymares varied.

Pity paid to see my dynamo
poised to rid us.

Cool chimes, a primal green
for studios.

Spur my clear plan astride
a stranger.

Cylinders versus diamonds
a decision.

Hollow, my grey ovule does
decide you.

Eternal, you beguile love or ruin – vocables.
Jejune vassals quote ten codas in reliquaries:
A (the ceaseless verses at occult monasteries;
requiems of dust, bound to nebulous particles:

Embers of gold); E (graven urns in sanctuaries;
brass bells, unsold, decreed priceless for our canticles);
I (a senseless verse – a spell, garbled in pentacles;
choruses, deemed perverse in desolate nurseries);

U (a universe, expressed as a murmur of tides,
all its perplexing maxims, exquisite suicides;
dim minds, transcended by vivid, hexadic prisms);

O (a vesper, stressing serenades or solitudes;
a clever muse, to generate endless interludes).
O, my elegiac ode, ends in paroxysms …

AEIOU

AOIEAIOUEUEOEUOEE
EIAIUEUEOUOAIAEAEE
AOIOEEUEOUEEAAE
UIOIEAUOUEUAEUUEE

OEOEEAEUEAEUEEEE
AEEAIEIEOIAIOOEE
IOUEAAEIEEEEEE
AAOEEOUEIEEEIEE

UEIEEIIEEIIE
AIEAIEEAIAUAIEIE
UEAIIEIIEAUAOUIEU

OUEEAIOEIEIEUEAE
IEEAEEEOEEEAE
OOEAAOIOEEEEU

AND SOMETIMES

SYZYGY PYX

GYP

GYPSY

PYGMY GYMS

JYNX SYNCH

TRY

PSYCH

TRYST PTYX

SYLPHS FLY

FLYBY

SKY

BY TSK TSK

SPY GLYPHS

LYSYL

BRR

GRR GLYCYL

NYM NYMPHS

WHY

WYRMS

HMM MY ZZZ

STY STYRYL

FRY

FYRDS

LYMPH CYST

WYRDS WYCH

LYNCH

WRY

MYTHY LYNX

MYST WYNDS

DRY

DRYLY

SHY BY SHH

CRY BY NTH

CWM

CRWTH

CRYPT STYX

MYTH HYMNS

THY

MYRRH

MY RHYTHMS

loveless vessels

we vow
solo love

we see
love solve loss

else we see
love sow woe

selves we woo
we lose

losses we levee
we owe

we sell
loose vows

so we love
less well

so low
so level

wolves evolve

H

for bpNichol

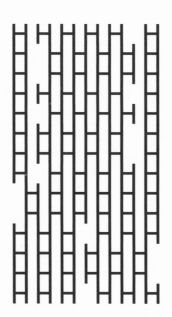

W

for Georges Perec

'To the V that stands for viewing what is all
around us, eyes turned outward, toward the
conscious surface of things, surrealism has
relentlessly opposed W.' – *André Breton*

'A meaningless distinction on W – leads to
automatic disqualification.' – *Georges Perec*

It is the V you double, not the U, as if to use
two valleys in a valise is to savvy the vacuum
of a vowel at a powwow in between sawteeth.

It is to ask the painter of a watercolour hue:
'why owe you twice what a sheep is or a tree,
if the fee you double has to hew you a puzzle?'

An enigma, like a game in E, its jigsaw zigzag
never fits the excess void left behind by X,
the exit on the way from 'why' to what is said.

If you glean an anagram from each angle, do you
dabble with your double view of what you hate:
a swastika that awaits your Olympiad of riddles?

Is this letter a residuum of what troubles you?
If you slice it down the middle, does it not
hereafter indicate a twofold victory over life?

If it maps the rise and fall of fortune, like a yo-yo,
why oh, why oh, must you find four palm trees
in a park, if not to make of them your symbol?

It is the name for an X whose V does not view
the surface of a lake but the mirror on a wall,
where U & you become a tautonym, a continuum.

EMENDED EXCESS

for Georges Perec

Czech pewterers mend pewter kettles; then the street sellers sell these mended vessels: ewers, cressets (even epergnes). Welsh veneerers mend veneer benches; then the street venders vend these mended effects: desks, dressers (even lecterns). When the Welshmen need new wrenches, the street peddlers get these men edgers, bevels, levels, levers (even tweezers); then the Welshmen re-mend the settees. The peddlers even peddle chessmen (hence, *les élèves d'échecs* get new chess sets, then referee the chess meets). The street sweepers sweep cement wherever renters rent the tenements.

When French jewellers embezzle De Beers, the stern execs there never detect the embezzlement; hence, the theft seems perfect. When the embezzlers resell these green gems (*les gemmes vertes*), the lensmen get themselves Fresnel lenses, then recheck the embezzled jewels; next the fences fence them. The resellers even peddle *les perles de mer* (eleven chests – seventeen pence per pellet). The mercers sell the well-kempt gents *les vêtements de Sèvres:* felt berets, kemp fezzes, tweed spencers, crewneck vests, serge breeches, cheverel belts. The well-dressed trendsetters set the trends.

When French gemsellers get served *les crevettes,* these
well-heeled gents expect *les entrées très excellentes:*
penne, green peppers, fennel, spelt, fresh cheeses,
rennet. When the Frenchmen get fed stewed greens
(beets, leeks, herbs), these trenchermen chew the beef
stew. The peelers peel twelve eggs; then the chefs
pestle the peeled eggshells; next, the blenders blend
les entremets éphémères; then the freezers freeze
les belles-Hélènes dégelées. The celebs get served *crêpe
de chèvre et crème de menthe* (never pretzels, never
seltzers). The sweeteners sweeten *les crèmes renversées.*

When French jetsetters hedge even bets, the lenders pledge these gents decent fees (three percent); then the tellers tender the checks; nevertheless, the spenders, when lent these shekels, spend, spend, spend (the spree never ends); hence, the feckless welshers never settle the debts. The expenses get deferred. The deferments get extended; nevertheless, the jerks renege; hence, the clerks send letters wherever these lendees dwell (Kent, Essex, Exeter, Bern, Ghent, Bergen – even Chester, even Dresden). The shredders shred the telexes (sent express); then the temps reshelve the emended ledgers.

When French embezzlers flee the scene, these perps rev the Mercedes-Benz, then speed (*beep, beep*). When the speeders veer, then swerve, Edsels, Vettes, even jeeps, get wrecked. When newsmen see the fender-bender, the news reps pre-empt the newsdesk, then re-tell the event; next, the newsreels present the weekend news. The Chechens secede. The Serbs get shelled. The Jews elect Knesset members, then resettle the Hebrew settlements. The elected Feds get re-elected – then we see the needless segments where the emcees peddle new detergents, new fresheners, even new repellents.

When freshmen get tested next semester, the nerds, the geeks (even the dweebs), reference dense exegeses (*les pensées des esthètes*): Hegel, Engels; Frege, Brecht – even Schlegel (hence, these teens get the best degrees). When presses present the next bestseller (Perec's *Les Revenentes*), the pressmen kern the lettered elements, then emend the text. The meddlers meddle. The spell-checker checks the lexemes, then respells them; hence, we see selected references get deleted (nevertheless, Perec's creed gets expressed; nevertheless, Perec's tenet gets preserved): E SERVEM LEX EST – *c'est le règlement.*

THE END

'The tedium is the message.'
– *Darren Wershler*

'Eunoia' is the shortest word in English to contain all five vowels, and the word quite literally means 'beautiful thinking'. *Eunoia* is a univocal lipogram, in which each chapter restricts itself to the use of a single vowel. *Eunoia* is directly inspired by the exploits of Oulipo (*l'Ouvroir de Littérature Potentielle*) – the avant-garde coterie renowned for its literary experimentation with extreme formalistic constraints. The text makes a Sisyphean spectacle of its labour, wilfully crippling its language in order to show that, even under such improbable conditions of duress, language can still express an uncanny, if not sublime, thought.

Eunoia abides by many subsidiary rules. All chapters must allude to the art of writing. All chapters must describe a culinary banquet, a prurient debauch, a pastoral tableau and a nautical voyage. All sentences must accent internal rhyme through the use of syntactical parallelism. The text must exhaust the lexicon for each vowel, citing at least 98% of the available repertoire (although a few words do go unused, despite efforts to include them: *parallax, belvedere, gingivitis, monochord* and *tumulus*). The text must minimize repetition of substantive vocabulary (so that, ideally, no word appears more than once). The letter Y is suppressed.

'Oiseau' (the French word for 'bird') is the shortest word in French to contain all five vowels. *Oiseau* pays tribute to the French precedents for *Eunoia*. 'Voyelles,' by Arthur Rimbaud, is the fabled French sonnet about the 'colours' of the vowels, and the English translation entitled 'Vowels' strives to convey both the meaning and measure of the original. 'Phonemes' is a homovocalic translation of 'Voyelles', preserving the original sequence of the vowels. 'Veils' is a homophonic translation of 'Voyelles', preserving the original voicing of the sounds. 'Vocables' is a perfect anagram of the French sonnet, and 'AEIOU' literalizes the title of 'Voyelles' by excising, from the poem, everything that is not a vowel.

'And Sometimes' itemizes every English word that contains only consonants. 'Vowels' is an anagrammatic text, permuting the fixed array of letters found in the title. 'H' is a visual sonnet constructed from the favourite letter of bpNichol – and the structure of this image is modelled upon the rhyme scheme found in the poem by Arthur Rimbaud. 'W' is an elegy for the favourite letter of Georges Perec, who (like bpNichol) admires one of the few consonants that can make a vowel sound. 'Emended Excess' exhausts vocabulary unsuitable for use in the retelling of the Iliad.

Eunoia has required years of perseverance to complete, and the book owes its success to the devoted support of many patient friends: Bruce Andrews, Derek Beaulieu, Charles Bernstein, Stan Bevington, Stephen Cain, Craig Dworkin, Kenneth Goldsmith, Scott Griffin, Neil Hennessy, Carl Johnston, Karen Mac Cormack, Steve McCaffery, Evan Munday, Christina Palassio, Marjorie Perloff, Rick/Simon, Brian Kim Stefans, Alana Wilcox and Suzanne Zelazo. Special thanks to Darren Wershler (who drove the car while I read Perec) and to Natalee Caple (who let me work while she slept). Thanks, as always, to Brigitte Schnell for her constant devotion.

Excerpts from this book have appeared over the years in the following magazines: *Arras, Big Allis, Blood and Aphorisms* (B+A), *The Capilano Review, Contemporary Verse 2* (CV2), *Geist, Harper's, Open Letter, Queen Street*

Quarterly and *Wordscapes*. Excerpts have also appeared in the following anthologies: *Blues and True Concussions: Six New Toronto Poets* (House of Anansi Press, 1996), *The Griffin Poetry Prize Anthology* (House of Anansi Press, 2002), *In Fine Form: The Canadian Book of Form Poetry* (Polestar, 2005), *Open Field: 30 Contemporary Canadian Poets* (Persea Books, 2005), *Af Ljóðum* (Nyhil Press, 2005), *Blue Light, Clear Atoms: Poetry for Senior Students* (Macmillan Education, 2006), *Nineteen Lines: A Drawing Center Writing Anthology* (Roof Books, 2007), *The Best American Poetry 2007* (Scribner Poetry, 2007), *The /n/oulipian Analects* (Les Figues Press, 2007), *The Reality Street Book of Sonnets* (Reality Street Editions, 2008), *Canadian Literature in English: Texts and Contexts* (Pearson Education, 2009) and *The Exile Book of Poetry in Translation: 20 Canadian Poets Take on the World* (Exile Editions, 2009).

115

Financial assistance has been kindly provided over the years by the Canada Council for the Arts, the Ontario Arts Council and the Toronto Arts Council. The epigraph by William Hayley owes its presence in this book to the gracious courtesy of Steve McCaffery.

Jack Spicer in 'Plato's Marmalade' (1960) prefigures the spirit of *Eunoia,* when he notes: 'A is a blank piece of driftwood being busted. E is a carpenter whose pockets are filled with saws, and shadows, and needles. I is a pun. O is an Egyptian tapestry remembering the glories of an unknown alien. U is the reverse of W. They are not vowels.'

FRONTISPIECE: 'Vowels Swivel' is a nested set of transparent geometric solids (each one generated by rotating a given vowel around a vertical axis): A (cone); E (cylinder); I (line); O (sphere); U (paraboloid).

Christian Bök is the author of *Crystallography* (Coach House Books, 2003), a pataphysical encyclopedia nominated for the Gerald Lampert Memorial Award for Best Poetic Debut. Bök has created artificial languages for two television shows: Gene Roddenberry's *Earth: Final Conflict* and Peter Benchley's *Amazon*. Bök has also earned acclaim for his virtuoso performances of sound poetry (particularly the *Ursonate* by Kurt Schwitters). His conceptual artworks (which include books built out of Rubik's Cubes and Lego Bricks) have been exhibited at galleries around the world. He teaches in the Department of English at the University of Calgary.

Typeset in Minion. Printed and bound
at Coach House Printing on bpNichol Lane

EDITORS
Darren Wershler and Alana Wilcox

DESIGNER
Christian Bök

COPYEDITOR
Alana Wilcox

Coach House Books
401 Huron Street (rear) on bpNichol Lane
Toronto, Ontario
M5S 2G5

416 979 2217
800 367 6360

mail@chbooks.com
www.chbooks.com